Fill In The Blanks

To Understanding The Kindle Fire

By Reginald T. Prior

Copyright © 2012 by Reginald T. Prior

Cover design by Reginald T. Prior
Book design by Reginald T. Prior

All rights reserved.

No part of this book may be reproduced in any form or by any electronic or mechanical means including information storage and retrieval systems, without permission in writing from the author. The only exception is by a reviewer, who may quote short excerpts in a review.

Reginald T. Prior

Visit http://www.rcsbooks.com or E-Mail me at reginaldprior@rcsbooks.com

Printed in the United States of America

First Printing: February 2012

ISBN - 978-1468191226

EAN - 1468191225

Trademarks And Copyrights

Trademarked and or copyrighted names appear throughout this book. Rather than list and name the entities, names or companies that own the trademark and or copyright or insert a trademark or copyright symbol for with every mention of the trademarked and or copyrighted name, The publisher and the author states that it is using the names for editorial purposes only and to benefit the trademark and or copyright owner, with no intentions of infringing on the trademark and or copyrights.

Warning and Disclaimer

Every effort has been made to make this book as complete and accurate as possible. No warranties are implied. The information provided is on a "as is" basis. The author and the publisher have no liability or responsibility to any individuals or entities with any respect to any loss or damages from the information provided in this book.

Preface

There are many books on the market that teach people how to use technology. But as I look through many of these books, I have found that they teach some of the basics, but miss a lot of critical things about how to fully utilize technology.

My aim of this book is to fill in these gaps that most books don't cover or spend sufficient time covering in common sense and in a way that is easily understood by everyone. As a computer technician for 12 years, I've come across many people that understand some things about technology, but want to have a better understanding about how it works and how to fully utilize them in their everyday lives.

In this book, I will be covering how to properly use Amazon's new hybrid tablet/E-Book reader, the Kindle Fire. At the time of the writing this book, The Kindle Fire is one of the best-selling E-Book readers of all time. You as the reader are the most important critics of this book. I value all of your feedback and suggestions that you may have for future books and other things that I can do to make these books better.

You can e-mail me at reginaldprior@rcsbooks.com and please include the book title, as well as your name and e-mail address. I will review your comments and suggestions and will keep these things in mind when I write future texts. Thank you in advance,

Reginald T. Prior

Acknowledgements

This book that you are reading right now takes a lot of time and sacrifice to put together. I would first and foremost thank God for giving me at the age of six the love of working on technology that still is as strong today as it was back then. I would like to thank my wife, Sharifa for being a trooper when I was spending many hours on my laptop putting this book together and also for being there to help me read my drafts to make sure that it would be understood.

Also I would like to thank my family and many friends that helped and supported me throughout the years on many other projects and being there for me in good times and bad. I hope that you all enjoy this book as much as I had putting it together.

Hello Everyone,

I would like to thank you in advance for purchasing "Fill In The Blanks To Understanding The Kindle Fire" I aim to make Amazon's Kindle Fire easy to learn while showing you the many features that Amazon has implemented to make the Kindle Fire one of the best-selling E-Book Reader/Tablets of all time.

Table Of Contents:

Chapter One: Touch Screen Computers Terminology Dictionary

Touch Screen Tablet Terminology Dictionary ------------------------------- 8
How To Turn Your Kindle Fire On And Off ------------------------------- 13
Putting Your Kindle Fire Into Sleep Mode ---------------------------------- 15
Setting Up Your Kindle Fire For The First Time ----------------------------- 15

Chapter Two: Getting To Know Your Kindle Fire

How To Unlock Your Kindle Fire --22
Navigating The Main Menu Screen --25
What Does All Of These Buttons On This Tablet Do? ----------------------29
Setting Options Through The Settings Menu -------------------------------30
How To Get Onto The Internet ---35
How To Setup And Use E-Mail --41
Sending Email From Your Tablet ---52
Deleting Email From Your Tablet ---54
How To Download & View Pictures On Your Tablet ------------------------55
Using The Gallery To Delete Pictures & Video--------------------------------63
How To Download Music To Your Tablet -------------------------------------67
Using The Music App To View And Play Your Music -----------------------81
Removing Music From Your Kindle Fire ---------------------------------------86

Chapter Three: How To Purchase Books & Magazines For Your Kindle Fire

How To Search For & Purchase Books And Magazines ---------------------88
How To Read Your Purchased Books And Magazines ---------------------93
Purchasing Non-Digital Items From Amazon With Your Kindle Fire ------97

Chapter Four: Using The Amazon App Store To Add Apps To Your Kindle

Getting To & Looking Through The Amazon App Store ---------------------99
Downloading And Installing Apps --101
Uninstalling Apps That You Don't Use ---105

Chapter Five: Tablet Security

Setting Up A Lock Screen And Wi-Fi Restriction Password -------------- 110

Chapter One:

Touch Screen Tablet Terminology Dictionary

Chapter One: Tablet Terminology Dictionary

Before we go into learning how to operate the Kindle Fire or any other tablet computer, I believe that before you can have knowledge about anything, you have to build your knowledge like a builder builds a house. First you have to lay a solid foundation down before we can start building floors and rooms within the house. Understanding the terminology and what it means is like laying the foundation on the house.

This chapter translates what we geeks talk about when we are talking about tablet devices. Decode the foreign language so to speak. This is not a full list of Tablet terminology, but this is a list of the most common terminology used for talking about most tablet computers. So with no further delays, let's get started laying the foundation to being confident to use your Kindle Fire tablet computer.

Note - When you go to purchase a Kindle Fire tablet computer, you would need to have an Amazon account already setup. Before we continue any further, if you don't already have an Amazon account, go to http://www.amazon.com and sign up for a FREE account.

As you go through signing up for your account, you will have the option of signing up for Amazon Prime. Amazon Prime is a membership program that gives you unlimited fast shipping, such as FREE Two-Day shipping to street addresses in the U.S. on all eligible purchases for an annual membership fee of $79.

Amazon Prime members in the U.S. can enjoy instant videos: unlimited, commercial-free, instant streaming of thousands of movies and TV shows through Amazon Instant Video at no additional cost. Members who own Kindle devices can also choose from thousands of books -- including more than 100 current and former New York Times Bestsellers

-- to borrow and read for free, as frequently as a book a month with no due dates, from the Kindle Owners' Lending Library.

Tablet Computers–

Tablet Computers are a category of mobile device that provides advanced capabilities beyond a typical laptop or other mobile devices. Tablets will have a touchscreen and run complete operating system software that provides a standardized look and feel.

QWERTY –

The term that commonly describes today's standard keyboard layout on English-language computers.

Accelerometer-

Sensors inside the tablet that measures tilt and motion. A device with an accelerometer knows what angle it is being held at. It can also measure movements such as rotation, and motion gestures such as swinging, shaking, and flicking.

One common use in tablets it to detect whether the tablet is upright or sideways and automatically rotate the graphics on the screen accordingly. Another common use is controlling games and other applications (such as music player) by moving or shaking the tablet.

Left And Right Swipe –

The action of touching the screen of the tablet and sliding your finger to the left for a Left Swipe, or to the right for a Right Swipe. Commonly used to navigate between screens on your tablet. The next pictures show examples of both left and right swiping.

Left Swiping

Right Swiping

<u>Up And Down Swipe –</u>

To touch the screen of the tablet and sliding your finger up for an Up Swipe, or down for a Down Swipe. Commonly used to show more options on a menu, or to navigate more of the webpage on your web browser.

Single/Double Tap –

To touch the screen of the tablet and quickly release once for single tap, twice for double tap. Commonly used to select or activate something. (Think of this as single or double clicking the mouse button on your computer)

Multi-Touch –

The ability for a touch surface to respond to multiple finger touches at the same time. For example, a common use for multi-touch is pinch-to-zoom, where you can place two fingers on a screen image (like photo, web page, or map) and spread your fingers to zoom in, or pinch your fingers together to zoom out.

Hardware

Hardware is the actual item or things that you can see and touch. Your Kindle Fire is considered hardware. Printers, scanners, mouse and keyboard are also considered hardware.

Applications/Apps

Applications or Apps are things you can buy and install that does a specific task. For example, your word processor like Microsoft Word, are apps designed to create documents. Microsoft's Internet Explorer® is an app designed for you to browse the Internet.

Norton Antivirus, AVG and McAfee are programs designed to protect your computer from viruses and malware, which are also programs designed to try to take control your computer or worse, look for information to steal your identity among other things.

Note – You need hardware and software working together to make your computer work. Just having one without the other is like having a car with no gas in it.

The Cloud or Cloud Computing

Cloud computing refers to applications and services offered over the Internet. These services are offered from data centers all over the world, which collectively are referred to as the "cloud." This metaphor represents the intangible, yet universal nature of the Internet.

Examples of cloud computing include online backup services, App Stores such as Google's Android Market, Apple's App Store or Amazon's App Store It also includes personal data services such as Apple's Mobile Me. Cloud computing also includes online applications such as Facebook.

WIFI –

Wireless networking technology using radio waves that provide a high-speed network and Internet connections over distances of a few hundred feet

3G-

3G Stands for 3rd-generation. Analog cellular phones were the first generation. Phones with text capabilities marked the second generation (2G). 3G is loosely defined, but generally includes high data speeds, streaming video and always-on data access, and greater voice capacity.

4G –

A somewhat vague term used to describe wireless mobile radio technologies that offer faster data rates than current 3G (third generation) technologies.

Turning On And Off Your Kindle Fire

The first thing that has to be done before we can start working with your Kindle Fire is to have it turned on. The power button is placed on the bottom of the tablet and looks like the next picture.

The one thing you need to keep in mind is that the power button has an icon that looks like the next picture:

To turn your tablet on, find the button that has the icon that looks like the picture shown above and press and hold down that button. After about 5 seconds, your tablet should turn on and then you can let go of that button.

To turn your Kindle Fire off, press and hold down the same button, and a menu choice will come up looking like the next picture:

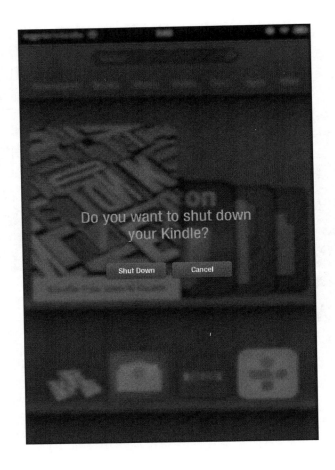

If you don't want to shut down, Single tap the "Cancel" button, and you will go back to the previous screen. If you want to shut down, Single tap the "Shut Down" button. Your Kindle Fire will then turn off.

Putting Your Kindle Fire Into Sleep Mode

You can put Kindle Fire to sleep mode while it is ON anytime. Just **press and release the power button** ⏻ to activate sleep mode on your Kindle Fire device.

Setting Up Your Kindle Fire For The First Time

Now after you have turned on your Kindle Fire for the first time, your device will boot up and the first time setup window will come up as shown in the next picture:

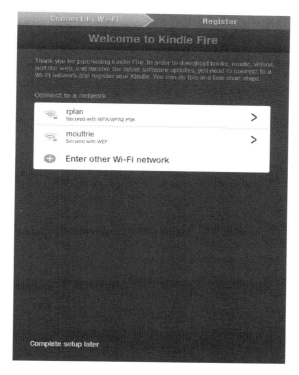

At this menu screen, you will be prompted to connect to your local WiFi hotspot. Single tap the one that you recognize and the prompt will come up asking you to enter the password for that hotspot. Enter the password through the touch keyboard, then single tap the "Continue" button.

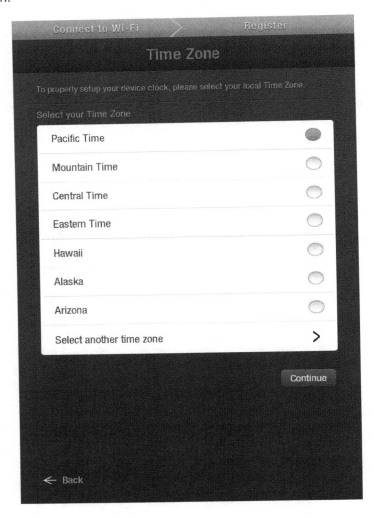

At this menu screen, The Kindle Fire setup asks you to set the time zone you currently reside in. Single tap the appropriate time zone and single tap the "Continue" button.

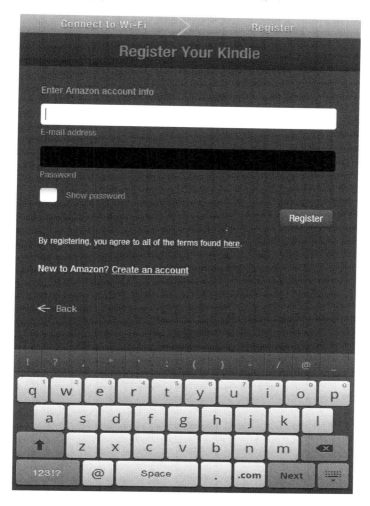

At this screen, you will enter your Amazon account username and password so that your Kindle Fire will sync with your Amazon account. Fill in the information by single tapping each textbox and using the touch keyboard to enter the appropriate information and single tap the "Register" button. Your Kindle Fire will then connect to your Amazon account and finish setup as shown in the next picture:

This is the final screen in the Kindle Fire setup menu. This screen lets you know that your Kindle is now registered and linked up with your Amazon account! Single tap the "Get Started Now" button to bring up the welcome screens as shown in the next pictures:

The previous set of pictures shows you a few quick tips on how to navigate the Kindle Fire's main screen. Single tap the "Next" arrow on the bottom right side of the screen twice and at the last screen, single tap the "Close" button to exit this quick overview of the Kindle Fire. We will go into this section more in depth in the next chapter in this book.

Chapter Two:

Getting To Know Your Kindle Fire

Over the years, trends in technology have changed. One trend was the shift from using desktop computers to notebook computers. This change happened because people had started to be more mobile and needed to use a computer on the go. So notebook computers became more popular than a desktop.

But for the past year or so, technology is currently in process of another trend happening. Tablet computers are suddenly able to do as much or more than a notebook computer, but in a smaller package. So more people are now swapping their notebooks for these powerful tablet computers.

This trend is going to continue to explode due to the fact that tablet computers and can do all of the same things as a notebook like sending and receiving email, playing games, surfing the Internet, and installing and running other applications.

After you have pushed the power button on your Kindle Fire and turned it on, your tablet will do a quick hardware check. After that check has completed, then you would setup your Kindle Fire for the first time as we covered in the previous chapter. After that, the your Kindle starts a "Master Program" called the operating system. This process is called booting up.

The booting up process is the act of the tablet setting up everything it needs to operate. Once your Kindle Fire has fully booted up, it will go right to the main screen where you would place your finger on the yellow slider icon and swipe left to unlock your Kindle Fire. The next picture shows what that screen looks like.

Before we go into actually using your Kindle Fire, first we will do a brief overview of the Kindle Fire. The Kindle Fire is a full color hybrid e-book reader/tablet version of Amazon's Kindle e-book reader. The Fire includes 8 GB of internal storage that can store about 80 applications, 10 movies, 800 songs or 6,000 books directly on the device for loading without an Internet connection.

But Amazon allows the device to have **unlimited** cloud storage for you to store music and other files to make up for the 8GB onboard storage. The only drawback of that is that you have to have a constant Internet connection to fully take advantage of loading additional content. That issue can easily be resolved by the use of a 3G or 4G MIFI device, available through your cellular phone provider. MIFI devices look similar to the next picture:

You would then connect the Fire to this device through WIFI (Explained in detail later in this book) and then you will have a constant Internet connection anywhere to enjoy additional content stored on the cloud. But if you don't have the need of having access to all of the content of the Fire on the go, then you can easily connect to the Internet through your local area hotspots or use your own wireless hotspot at home.

Navigating The Main Kindle Fire's Main Screen

After you have swiped to unlock your Kindle Fire, you will be presented with the home screen. In the following sections, we will go over in detail everything you see on the main screen of your Kindle Fire. The next picture shows the most important things to keep in mind when you look at the main screen on your Kindle Fire:

- The Notification Menu Section displays important information such as when you receive new mail, system or application updates. It states your username's Kindle with a number after that, representing how many notifications you currently have. When you Single tap on the word "Kindle" to show this information, The notification menu will come up similar to the next picture:

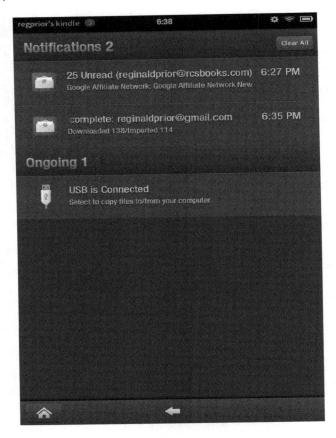

To go back to the previous screen, single tap the left arrow or the home button on the bottom of this screen.

- The Quick Settings Section displays information including the time, battery status, signal strength and other information. When you single tap on this section, additional options show up where it shows additional settings as shown In the next picture:

- The Navigation Bar provides shortcuts to all of your digital content stored on the Kindle. Every shortcut has a purpose such as:

    Newsstand – Being the place where you would purchase and read digital versions of magazines & newspapers

    Books – Being the place where you would purchase and read Electronic Books

    Music – Being the place where you would purchase and listen to your music on your Kindle Fire

    Videos – Being the place where you would view and purchase videos from Amazon's Library of instant videos to your Kindle Fire

    Docs – You can view your personal documents on your Kindle Fire in this section. You and others can e-mail personal documents to your Kindle through your Send-to-Kindle e-mail address (Which is shown when you open this section). You must ensure that you have approved the sender's e-mail address through your Manage Your Kindle webpage located at (https://www.amazon.com/manageyourkindle) and your document is supported file type (Pictures, PDF's & Microsoft Office Documents)

Apps – Being the place where you would purchase and open apps that are on your Kindle Fire

Web – Being the place where you would surf the Internet using Amazon's Silk web browser

- The Carousel Section allows you to quickly go through your recent apps and books to quickly go back into them without searching for them in each one of the navigation bar menus. Swipe left or right to go through the items on this list and single tap on one to open it.

- The Favorite Items Section allows you single tap an icon to start a specific application or book. Think about this as a shortcut on your Windows or Macintosh computer. To add an item to the shortcut menu, single tap and hold it down on an icon, app or a book and a menu will pop up as shown in the next picture:

Single tap the "Add To Favorites" menu choice, and that specific app or book icon will be placed in the Favorites section.

What Does All Of These Buttons Do On The Kindle?

Before we go into actually using your Kindle Fire, first we have to go over the function buttons and fully explain they are used for, because you will use them a lot. These buttons are usually located at the bottom of the screen, and look similar to the next picture:

- This is the back button on your Kindle fire. This button is used for multiple functions. One function of this button is to go back to a previous screen within the Kindle or a previous webpage when surfing the Internet.

- This is the home button on your Kindle fire. This button is used to take you back to the home screen from anywhere.

- This is the menu key. This is one of the most important functionality keys on the Kindle Fire. This key is most commonly used to provide additional options for your Kindle or within an application. Think of this button as your "File" menu within any Windows program. This icon will show up only when there are additional options for that particular application.

- This button is your search button. Single tap the magnifying glass icon and type in the dialog box to do a app, document or web search at the same time on your Kindle.

Note – Sometimes when you are in a app or on some menus, the function buttons will hide and look similar to the next picture:

You would then single tap the up arrow symbol to show the navigation buttons again.

Setting Options For Your Kindle Through The Settings Menu

There are times when you want to change the way your tablet operates. You would to go to the settings menu to accomplish this. The settings menu at first glance can be very intimidating because there are so many options. But we only need to be concerned with a couple of selections at this time.

To get to the settings menu, on the home screen (You would get to the home screen from anywhere on your Kindle by pressing the "Home" key on your tablet. It would look like this) Then single tap the "Quick Settings" section on the top right of the main menu screen. When you single tap on this section, additional options show up where you have additional settings as shown in the next picture:

Single tap the "More" icon and the settings screen should look like the next picture:

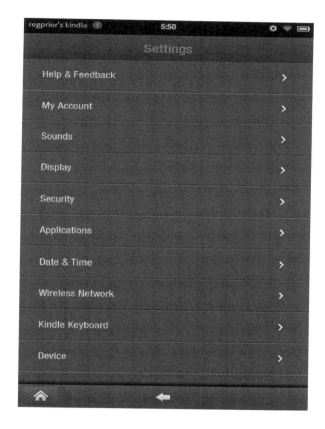

Like I had mentioned earlier in this section, the settings menu can be intimidating, but we need to only at this time be concerned with only a few options here:

1. Wireless Network Settings – This is the section where you can change the hotspot your tablet connects to. Single tap this menu and all of the area hotspots will come up as shown in the next picture:

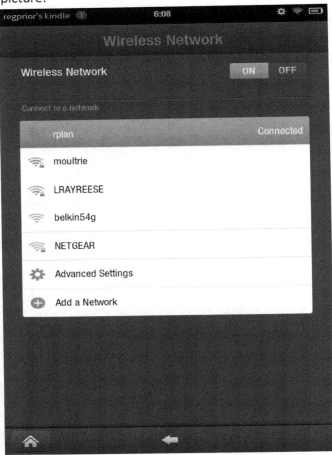

Single tap the one that you recognize and the prompt will come up asking you to enter the password for that hotspot. Enter the password through the touch keyboard, then single tap the "Connect" button and your Kindle will then connect to that hotspot.

2. Sounds– This is the section where you can change the notification sounds for events that happen on your tablet.

Single tap that menu selection to go into that menu. Your screen should look like the next picture:

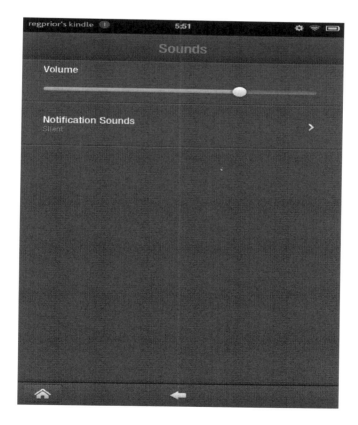

In this menu, a lot of the menu choices are self-explanatory. To increase or decrease the volume, you would slide the white slider to the left to decrease the volume, and to the right to increase the volume. To change the notification sound for your tablet, single tap the "Notification Sounds" option and a dialog box will come up, showing all of the notification tones that are available on your tablet. It will look like the next picture:

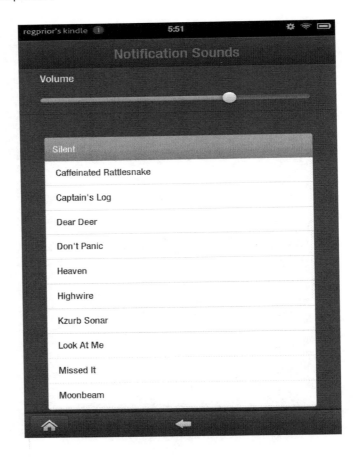

Swipe up or down through selection of notification tones. Select one by single tapping on it and a sample sound will play. If you like it, single tap the left arrow button at the bottom of this menu and that notification ringtone will be set on your Kindle, or press the left arrow button without single tapping on anything and nothing would be changed.

How To Get Onto The Internet

One of the best aspects about having a tablet is having the ability to surf the internet just about the same way as you would on a computer or a laptop. To go onto the Internet, You will have to launch the browser application.

You will do that by single tapping the "Web" option on the navigation bar on the home screen (You would get to the home screen from anywhere in on the tablet by pressing the home key. It look like this) When you are there Single tap the words "Web" on the navigation bar. The Kindle web browser will come up like the next picture:

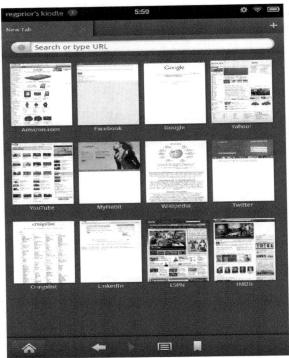

To go to a different webpage other than the one that comes up by default, swipe down to go to the top of the current webpage, and the address bar will come up as shown in the next picture:

Single tap inside the address bar and then the touch keyboard will show up where you can type the address of the webpage you wish to go to. While you are typing in the webpage address, a live Google search is being conducted behind the scenes were your desired website may come up. You can single tap on that address if it does come up. An example of this happening is shown on the next picture:

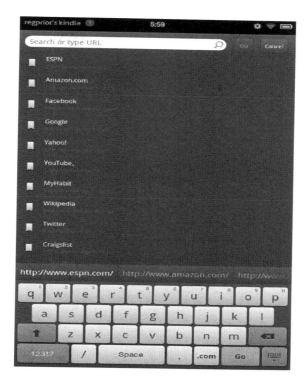

When you are done typing in the desired website, then single tap the "Go" button, and you will be taken to that webpage. Just like the web browser on your computer, you can set various options such as the default search engine among other things.

To show the browser options, while having the Kindle browser open, press the menu key on your tablet at the bottom of the screen which looks like this . The option menu will come up like the next picture.

Next, single tap the "Settings" option. The screen will come up looking similar to the next picture:

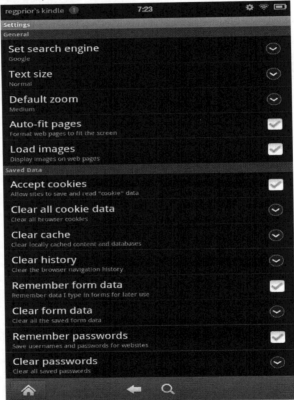

To change the search engine, single tap the "Set Search Engine" option and the set homepage screen will come up like the next picture:

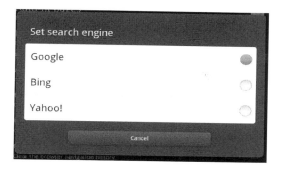

Single tap the desired search engine you wish your Kindle to use and the new default search engine will be set to the one you just tapped. You can do other things in the Kindle web browser such as bookmarking a favorite webpage. To bookmark a webpage, first, go to the webpage you want to bookmark, then press the menu key on your tablet at the bottom of the screen which looks like this 🔲. The option menu will come up like the next picture.

Single tap the "Add Bookmark" option and the add bookmark prompt will come up like the next picture:

39

To add the bookmark to your bookmarks list, single tap the "Ok" button and the bookmark will be added to your main browser screen.

To view all of your bookmarks, single tap the bookmark ribbon to the right of the address bar which would look similar to this . The bookmarks menu will come up looking similar to the next picture:

To go to a specific bookmark, single tap the specific bookmark and the browser will then go to that website.

How To Setup And Use E-Mail

Electronic Mail or E-Mail has forever changed how people communicate from the business world, to families that live far away so that they can easily stay in touch. E-Mail allows you not only to send letters to people, but also you can send pictures and other things.

Note – If you have a Gmail, Aol, Yahoo or Hotmail account, you can use that account with your Kindle Fire. If you wish to use an email account from your Internet Service Provider for your home computers, you can also use that account with your Kindle Fire.

But before we get into using your email account on your Kindle Fire, first we would have to Configure Your Kindle to work with the E-Mail address your Internet Service Provider has given you to use. The 4 things we will need to get your E-Mail to work are listed below:

1. Your Internet Service POP Server address (POP stands for Post Office Protocol). It handles E-Mail coming in from people that has sent you E-Mail.

2. Your Internet Service SMTP Server address (SMTP stands for Simple Mail Transfer Protocol). This is used to send messages and forwards that you have written to people.

3. The username you gave the Internet service provider to setup your Internet account with them.

4. Also the password that you gave the Internet service provider to setup your Internet account with them.

If you don't remember or lost the documentation that they gave to you, you are going to have to call the customer service line of the Internet Service Provider that you are using to get this information, because you are going to need it to get your Kindle to send and receive E-Mails at all. When you have this information, we can move on to the next step: setting up the e-mail program itself.

To setup the e-mail account from your Internet Service Provider, Single tap the Apps icon the navigation bar on the home screen (You would get to the home screen from anywhere on your Kindle by pressing the home key on your tablet. It look like this) On the home screen, single tap the "Apps" wording on the navigation bar. The apps screen will come up like the next picture:

Swipe up or down to find the Mail application icon. Single tap the Mail app icon, which icon looks like the next picture

And the Email Application will come up and Your screen should look like the next picture:

Single tap the orange "Start" button to get started.

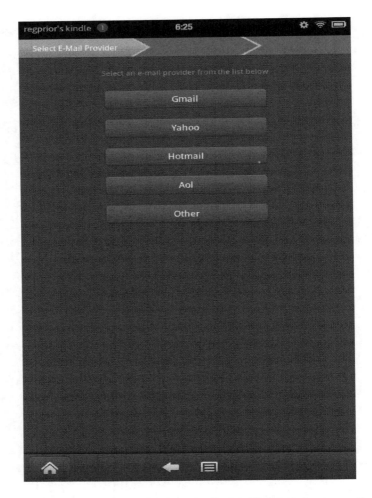

This screen is the first step in the Kindle Mail® wizard where they ask you what email service you wish to set up. As stated earlier in this section, you can use other types of email such as AOL, Gmail or any other web-based email service with your Kindle. If you wish to use one of those email accounts, just single tap the appropriate service, enter your username and password and go through the wizard to set up your email. Then you can skip ahead to page 52.

But in this example, we are using an email address that your Internet service provider gave to us to use with our home computers. To setup that account, single tap the "Other" button and the setup screen will come up like the next picture:

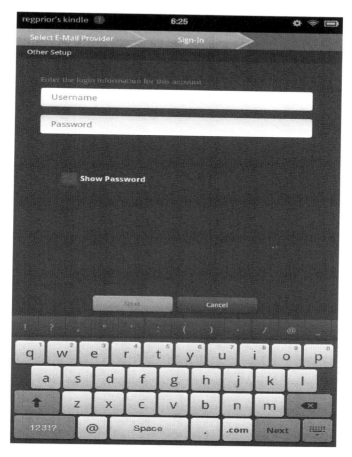

This screen is the second step in the Kindle Mail® wizard where they ask you to type in e-mail address and your password in the text boxes. Single tap the username box, And the touch keyboard comes up. Type in the e-mail address your Internet Service Provider has given you. It is usually username@internetprovidername.com .org or .net. Then single tap the password box, type in your password, then single tap the "Next" button on the tablet screen.

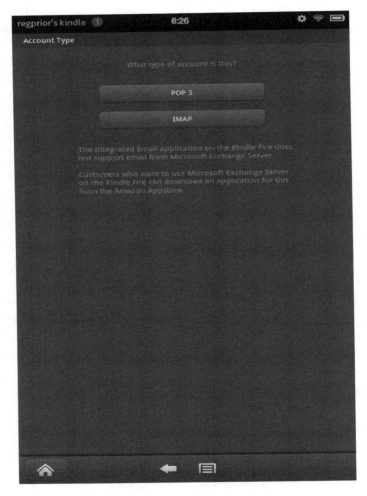

This screen is the step where they ask you to specify the type of email that you are using. In most cases, it would be POP mail, so single tap the "POP3" button.

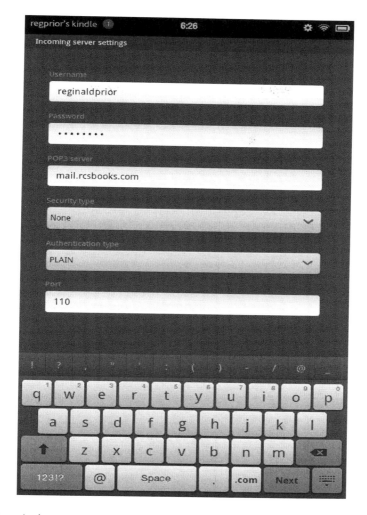

In this window, we are going to type in the POP (Incoming) server information from your Internet Service Provider so the program could connect to the right servers to deliver and to send E-Mail. Single tap the POP3 Server textbox and the touch keyboard will come up.

Type your pop server address in the POP3 server box, then single tap the password text field, type in your password, swipe up on the screen and single tap the orange next button.

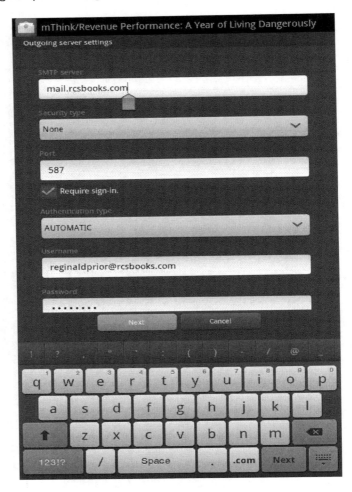

In this window, we are going to type in the SMTP server information from your Internet Service Provider. Single tap the SMTP Server textbox and the touch keyboard will come up.

Type your server address in the SMTP server box, then single tap the password text field and type in your password, then single tap the orange next button.

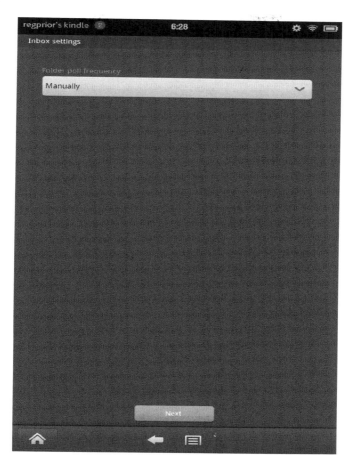

This screen shows additional options you can set for this email account such as the time interval that the Kindle will check for new email messages. Single tap the drop box if you want to change the default options, otherwise single tap the "Next" button.

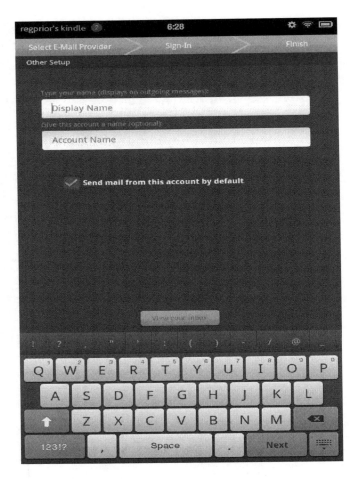

This screen is where you can set up a specialized name for this E-Mail box. Also in this menu, you would type in your name or a name you want people to see when they receive emails you send from this tablet. Fill in this information and single tap the "View Your Inbox" button.

Your Kindle Fire will now attempt to connect to the email service using the information you typed in. And if the attempt was successful, then the program will start downloading email as shown in the next picture:

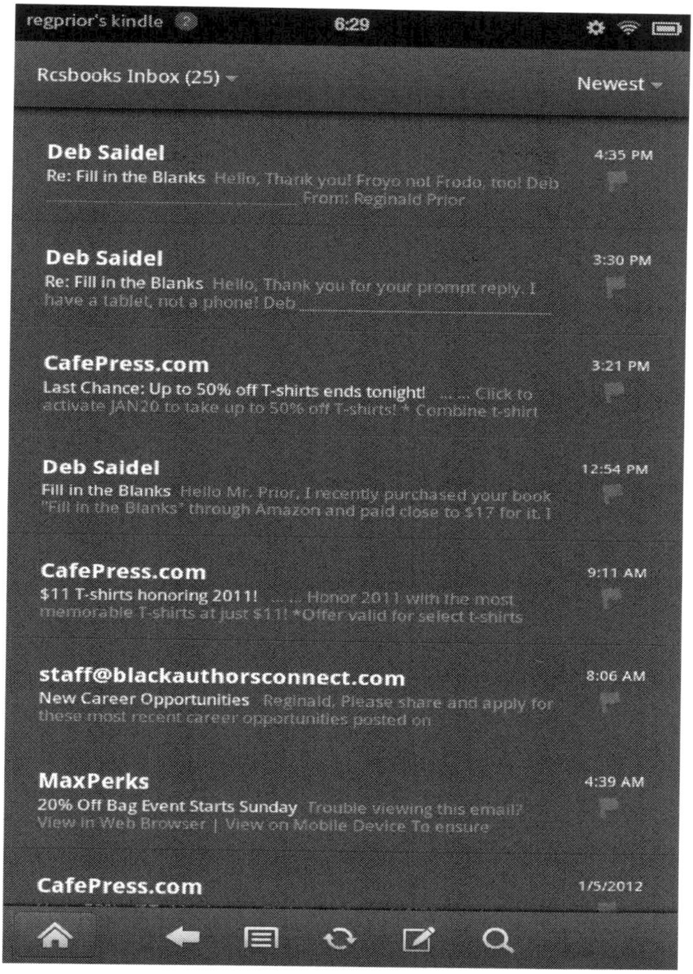

And your email is now setup and ready to go!

Sending E-Mail From Your Tablet

To send email using your tablet, you would have to go back into Kindle Mail by single tapping the apps wording from the navigation bar on the home screen (You would get to the home screen by pressing the home key on your tablet. It look like this) swipe up or down to find the Kindle Mail application. Single tap the icon that looks like the next picture:

And the Android Mail app will load and check for new Emails and will look like the next picture:

To start composing a new email message, Single tap the "Compose" icon located in the bottom part of the screen which looks like this  The new message window will then come up and looks similar to the next picture

To create a message, have the person's e-mail handy. Make sure the spelling of the e-mail is correct because your message will not be sent at all if the spelling is incorrect. The steps below are how you would compose the e-mail in Kindle mail.

1. First, single tap the "To:" textbox. The touch screen keyboard will come up. Type the e-mail address of the person that you want to send this message to in the textbox. Again, make sure that the e-mail address is correctly spelled, or the message will not be sent at all.

2. Secondly, single tap the "Subject:" textbox. Type a brief summary of what this e-mail is about in the textbox.

3. Thirdly, single tap the Message Text textbox on the bottom of the window. Type the actual message in this box.

4. When you are done typing your actual message to this recipient of this message, single tap the orange send button on the bottom part of this screen. Your E-Mail message will then be sent to the e-mail address you inputted. That is how you put together and send an e-mail message in Kindle mail.

Deleting Messages In Kindle Mail

To delete email messages on Kindle mail, you would have to go back into Kindle Mail by single tapping the apps wording from the navigation bar on the home screen (You would get to the home screen by pressing the home key on your tablet. It look like this) and swipe up or down to find the Kindle Mail application. Single tap the icon that looks like the next picture:

Email

On the main screen, swipe up or down to find the message you wish to delete, and single tap the message to open it. When the message is open, you will notice a trash can icon at the bottom of the message as shown in the next picture:

To delete this message, simply single tap the garbage can icon located at the bottom part of the screen and the message will be deleted from your tablet.

How To Download Pictures To Your Tablet

Many people have pictures on their computer that they may want to show to other people or view from time to time. You could get one of those keychain digital photo frames that look like the next picture:

But the truth of the matter is that the quality of the pictures downloaded to the frame leaves a lot to be desired and also the software on some of them that are used to download pictures to them are not the easiest to use. The more logical solution is to use your tablet as a portable picture frame. The way to download pictures off of your computer to your Kindle tablet cannot be any simpler than the instructions we are about to get into now.

To transfer your pictures from your computer to your Kindle Fire, First Plug your Kindle Fire into your computer using a micro usb cable. These cables usually come with many cell phones. When you plug your kindle into your computer, the main screen of your Kindle Fire will look like the next picture:

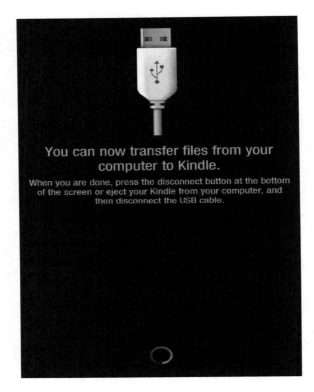

I suggest that if you don't already have Google's Picasa installed on your computer, that you download and install it from http://www.picasa.com. This program will help you easily interface with your Kindle. After you have downloaded and installed Picasa onto your computer, the installer will leave an icon on your desktop you would double left click on to open the program. The icon looks like this:

After you double left click on the icon shown above, Picasa will then open up to the main screen that will look like the next picture:

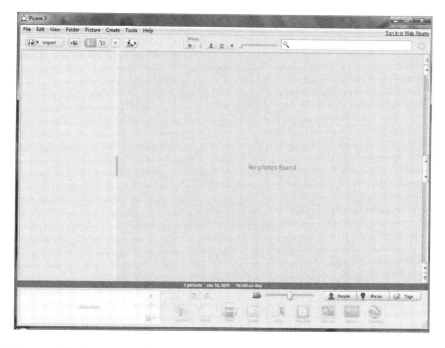

Picasa will then search your computer for pictures then load and organize them on this main screen. As you can see, Picasa is divided into several parts. We will go over each part in detail in the next section.

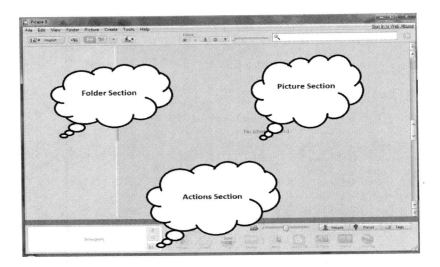

Picture Section - This is the section where previews of pictures will show up when you single left click on a folder in the folder section.

Folder Section – This is the section where you will organize your pictures into albums for easy and quick access.

Actions Section – This is the section where you would tell Picasa what you want to do with a picture or album you have selected.

To transfer pictures to your Kindle Fire, simply select one of your pictures from an album by single left clicking the picture in the picture section, and holding the left mouse button down. Drag the picture down to the selection tray in the action section of the main window and let go of the left button on your mouse. It looks like the next picture:

When you let go of your mouse button, your picture should then appear in this window with a green circle on the photo looking like the picture below:

This will let you know that the picture was successfully inserted into the selection tray. Then go through the rest of your albums and select other pictures you wish to print and put them into the selection tray the same way. When you are done selecting pictures and want to transfer them to your Kindle, single left click the export button on the actions section. The export menu will come up looking like the next picture:

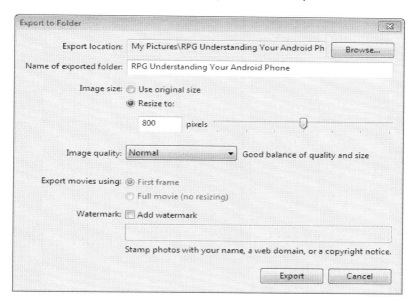

When this menu choice comes up, you are going to have to change the Export location field to be the drive letter of your Kindle Fire's memory card. To do that, single left click the "Browse" button and the menu prompt will come up like the next picture:

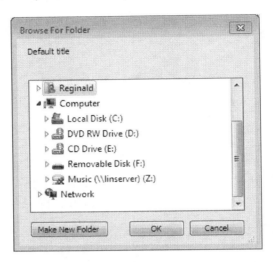

Single left click the arrow right next to the computer label and all of the drives on your computer will show up like the picture shown above. In this case, the Kindle Fire's drive letter is the (F:/) drive, so we would single left click the arrow next to the (F:/) drive once, find the "Pictures" folder, then single left that folder, then single left click the "OK" button to select it. Your computer screen should look similar to the next picture:

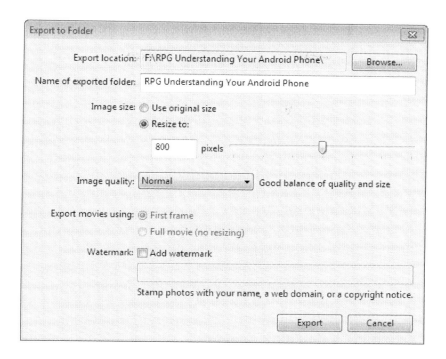

At this point, you could single left click the "Name of exported folder" text field and give this album a different name, or you could leave it as is. Now you would transfer the pictures to your Kindle by single left clicking on the "Export" button. Your pictures will now transfer to your Kindle.

When you are done copying all of the pictures that you want to your tablet, disconnect the USB cable from your computer and then you should be able to single tap the gallery app in the apps section on the navigation pane on the home screen which icon looks like the next picture:

And the pictures should sync up where you can single tap on them to show up full screen on your tablet as shown in the next picture. I previously had uploaded a folder called "Test Pictures" to my Kindle, as you can see it below in the gallery.

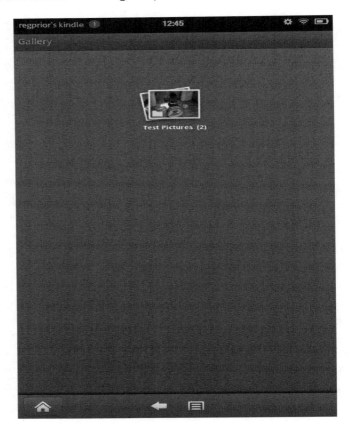

Single tap on that album, and all the pictures in that album would show up on the screen. You can show your downloaded pictures in a slideshow by single tapping one of the pictures, then single tapping the slide show icon in the bottom part of the screen which would look similar to the next picture:

Your pictures in that album will then show in a slideshow.

Note – You can press the left arrow button anytime during the slide show to end the slide show.

Using The Gallery To Delete Pictures

There are times when you want to remove a picture from your tablet to free up memory on your tablet. To delete a picture or video clip from your tablet, open the Gallery app from the apps menu on the navigation bar on the home screen (You would get to the main screen by pressing the home key on your tablet. It look like this ) swipe up or down to find the gallery app as shown in the next picture.

Single tap the icon and your pictures will show up where you can left or right swipe in the gallery and single tap a album to show pictures as shown in the next picture:

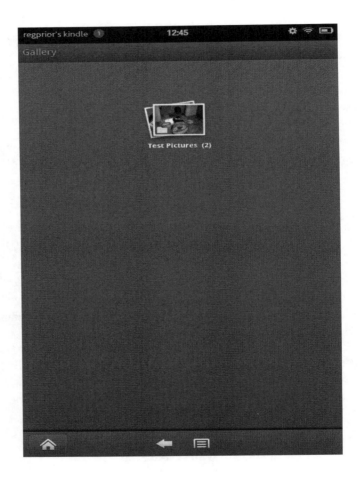

To delete a picture on your Kindle, first open the album where the picture is located by swiping left or right through that gallery and single tapping the album to show all of the pictures in the album as shown in the next picture:

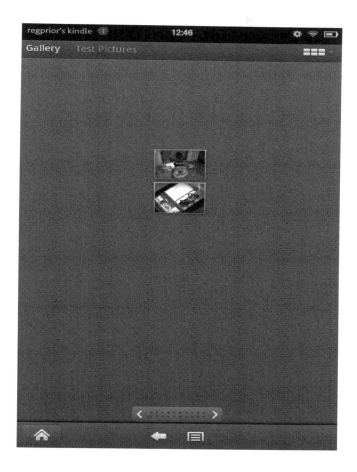

To select a picture to delete, single tap and hold on the picture until a green checkmark appears on the picture as shown in the next picture:

At the bottom part of the screen, you will notice a garbage can icon which looks like this:

Single tap that icon and a menu will come up asking you to confirm deleting this picture as shown in the next picture

Single tap the "Confirm Delete" button and the picture will be deleted from your tablet.

How To Download Music To Your Kindle

You can download music to your Kindle Fire two ways – Either purchasing them from the Amazon MP3 store or by transferring MP3 files to your Kindle from to your computer. We are going to cover both methods of getting your music on your Kindle Fire. The first method we are going to cover is how to purchase music from Amazon's Music Store.

To get to Amazon's Music Store, single tap the "Music" link on the notification bar on the home screen, and the music section will open like the next picture:

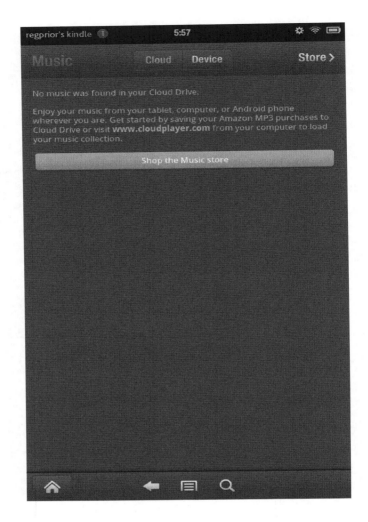

On the top right section of this screen, single tap the "Store" link to be taken to the Amazon's Music Store. When you do this, the Amazon Music store will come up as shown in the next picture:

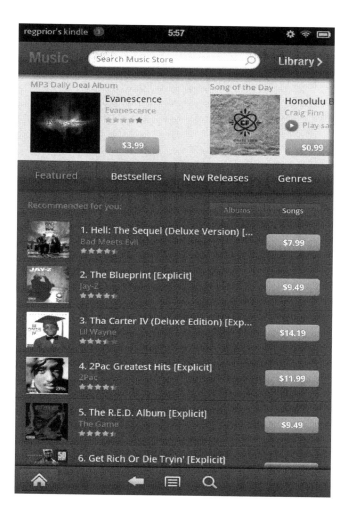

As you can see, the music is organized by featured artist, bestsellers and other categories. If you want to search for a specific artist, single tap the textbox at the top of the screen where it says "Search Music Store" and the touch keyboard will show. Type in the album title or artist you want to search for, then single tap the search button and the results will show as shown in the next picture:

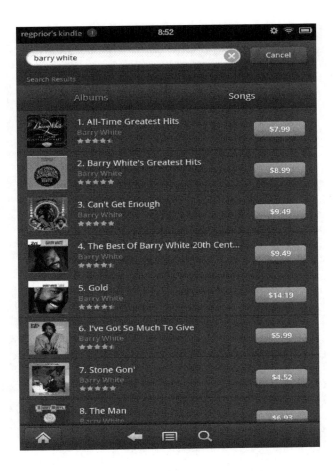

To purchase a specific album, single tap the yellow button next to the album twice, and the album will download and install to your cloud drive where you can play them from the Music section.

But before we go any further, if you are reading this book and happen to be setting up your Kindle Fire for the first time, when you try to purchase an song, a prompt will pop up stating that you have to link your Kindle to a card through your Amazon account to utilize the One-Click setting as shown in the next picture:

This is a one-time configuration step. After setting this up, you will not see this prompt again. Single tap the blue "Click Here" link and your Kindle Fire's web browser will come up asking you to sign into your Amazon account as shown in the next picture:

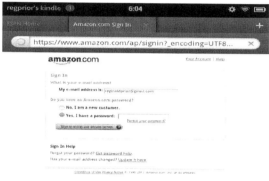

Enter your E-Mail address and password and single tap the yellow "Sign In Using Our Secure Server" button and you will be brought to the second step in setting up a card through Amazon.

As you can see in this step, you have to setup this Kindle for One-Click Payments. Single tap the blue "Edit" link to get started doing this.

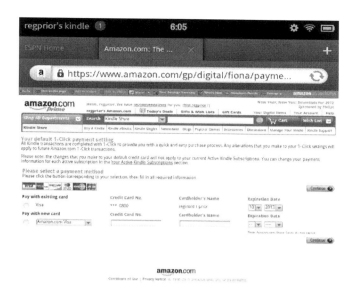

On this screen, if you already have a card on file with Amazon, you can single tap the bubble next to the card you wish to use and single tap the orange "Continue" button. But if you want to add a specific card for use with your Kindle Fire, then you can enter your information under the "Pay with new card" section and single tap the orange "Continue" button.

This window lets you know that the One-Click payment method is all set for this Kindle. You can now single tap the home button to go back to the home screen, then single tap the "Music" wording on the navigation bar, and single tap the "Store" wording to get back to the Amazon's Kindle store to purchase music.

The second way to get music on your Kindle is to transfer music from your computer to your device. The first thing you have to do is to connect your Kindle to your computer by plugging one end of a microusb cable (Usually Comes with any cell phone made within the last two years) into your Kindle and the other end into a USB port on your computer. Then your computer will show your Kindle as a separate hard drive device as shown in the next picture:

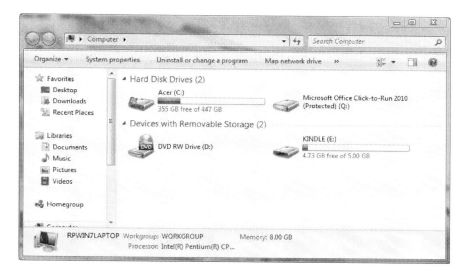

But before we can transfer music to your Kindle Fire, we first would have to download music from your music CD's to your computer. And to do that, get your favorite music CD's together to import into your computer. If you already have music downloaded to Windows Media Player, then feel free to skip ahead to page 79.

Open up Windows Media Player to the main screen and insert one of your music CD's into your computer. Windows Media Player will read the CD and the songs from the CD will appear in the song list section of the program as shown in the next picture:

The next step to transferring a music CD to your computer is first making sure that Windows Media Player transfers the music to your computer into the MP3 format. This format is most compatible with your tablet.

And how to do that depends on which version of Windows Media Player you have installed on your computer. In Windows Media Player 11, which is installed for Windows XP and Vista, move your mouse cursor to the down arrow under the "Rip" button and single left click on it. A submenu will show up as shown in the picture below.

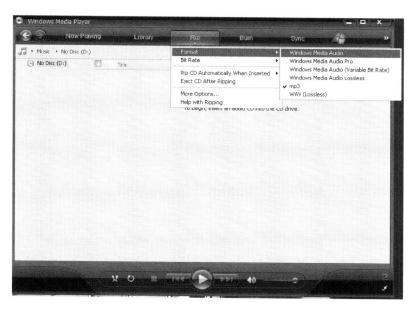

Windows Media Player 11 Screen

Under the format submenu, make sure you have the MP3 format check marked as shown in the previous picture. With Windows Media Player Version 12, which is only for Windows 7 at the time of the writing of this book, single left click the "Rip Settings" button. Under the format submenu, make sure you have the MP3 format check marked as shown in the next picture:

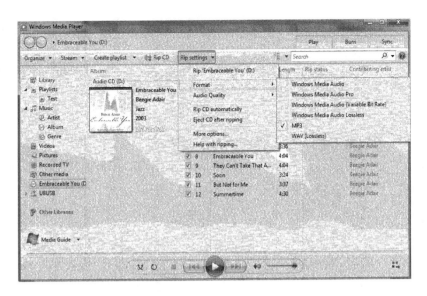

Windows Media Player 12 Screen

After that, single left click the CD icon on the library section of Windows Media Player. The songs on the CD will appear in the songs list section with a check mark next to each one of them. If you want all of the songs on this CD to be transferred to the computer, leave the check marks there. If not, uncheck the songs you don't want to transfer by single left clicking the check mark of each song to unselect them from the transfer list.

When you're ready to download the music CD, single left click the "Rip" button. Then the music will be downloaded to your computer. Repeat the last instructions for each additional CD you want to import into your computer to transfer to your tablet.

The next step in the process to play your music on your Kindle Fire is to actually transfer music from your computer to your tablet. And to do that, first single left click the arrow next to the music menu in the Library section on the main menu. A submenu will come up with three choices, Artist, Album & Genre. Single left click on Artist.

All of the music that you have downloaded onto your computer will come up in the song list section, arranged by Artist. Double left click an artist to show songs and individual albums you have from that artist on your computer. To transfer an individual song to your tablet, move your mouse cursor to the song and single left click and hold the left mouse button down.

Drag the song to the sync list where it says "Drag Items Here" and let go of the left mouse button. Repeat for each song you want to transfer. Then move your mouse cursor to the "Start Sync" button and single left click on it to transfer the music to your tablet.

To transfer a complete album, move your mouse cursor to the album cover and single left click and hold the left mouse button down. Drag the album cover to the sync list and let go of the left mouse button. Repeat for each album you want to transfer. Then move your mouse cursor to the "Start Sync" button and single left click on it to transfer to your Android tablet.

When you are done copying all of the music that you want to your tablet, disconnect the USB cable from your computer and then the music transferred to your tablet will be ready for playing.

Using The Music App To View And Play Your Music

In the previous section, "How to Download Music to Your Tablet" we went over how to transfer music from your personal CD's to your computer and from there, onto your tablet. Now you want to play them on your tablet. You would do that using the music app.

It is located on the main screen on the navigation bar. You would get to the main screen by pressing the home key on your tablet. It looks similar to this)

After you get to the home screen, on the navigation bar, you should see the words "Music". Single tap on it and the music screen should come up as shown in the next picture:

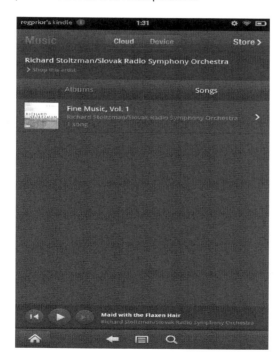

When you open the music section of your Kindle Fire, your downloaded and cloud-based music should show up where you can single tap on them to play on your tablet as shown in the next picture.

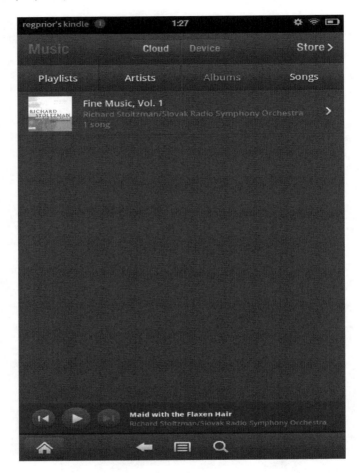

To see the song list from a particular artist, single tap the artist button, then single tap that artist's name. In this case, I will tap the artist Richard Stolzman. Then all of the albums that I have downloaded from Richard Stolzman will come up as shown in the next picture:

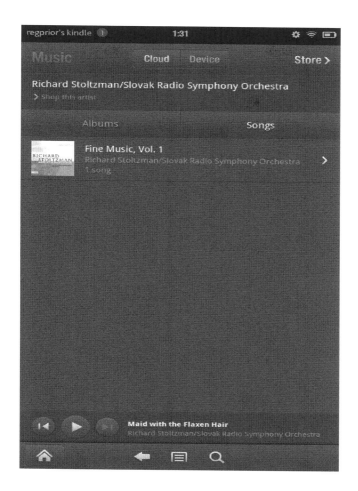

To see the songs from a particular album, single tap the album and the song list will show as shown in the next picture:

When the song list comes up, you can swipe up or down to view all of the songs and then single tap a song to play it. When you do that, your screen will look like the next picture:

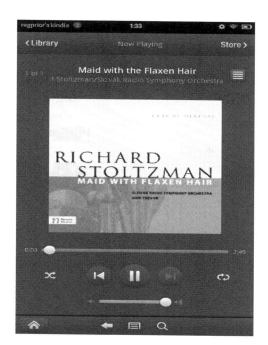

On this screen, you can rewind, pause and go to the next song by tapping on the appropriate buttons. The buttons are shown below:

This button is the pause/play button. When the song is currently playing, this button will turn to the pause symbol. When a song is paused, then this button will turn to the play symbol.

This button is to cycle to the next song on the current play list.

This button is to go back to the previous song on the play list.

To go back to the main music screen, press the left arrow button on your Kindle, then you would go back to the song list.

Note – If you want to delete a song from your tablet, while under the song list section, single tap and hold your finger on the particular song, and the song menu will come up as shown in the next picture.

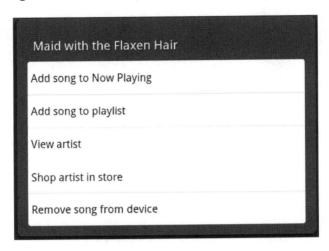

Single tap the "Remove Song From Device" menu choice, and a menu prompt will come up making sure that you want to delete this particular song as shown in the next picture:

Single tap the "Yes" button, and the song will be deleted from your Kindle.

Chapter Three: How To Purchase Books & Magazines To Read On Your Kindle

How To Purchase Books & Other Content From The Kindle Store

The Kindle line of E-Book readers in the past has always allowed you to purchase and read various types of content with simplicity and ease. That doesn't change with the Fire, but the only difference is that you can now enjoy content in full, vibrant color.

To Purchase Books to read on your Kindle, on the home screen single tap the "Books" wording from the menu on the navigation bar on the home screen (You would get to the main screen by pressing the home key on your tablet. It look like this) The books menu will show up as shown in the next picture:

As you can see, I have already purchased a few books along with the one example that comes with the Kindle, which is the Oxford American Dictionary. To go to the Kindle store to purchase and download more books, just single tap the "Store" wording at the top right part of the screen, and you will then go to the Kindle store as shown in the next picture:

As you can see, books are organized by the top 100 and other categories. If you see something that interests you, just single tap on it and the book description will come up similar to the next picture:

To purchase this book, single tap the "Buy for $x.00" button twice and the book will be purchased through your card that you attached to your Amazon account and download to your Kindle. But if you want to read a sample before buying, double tap that button twice and a sample copy will then be downloaded to your Kindle.

If you want to search for a specific title or author, single tap the textbox at the top of the screen where it says "Search Book Store" and the keyboard will show. Type in the title or author you want to search for and the results will show as shown in the next picture:

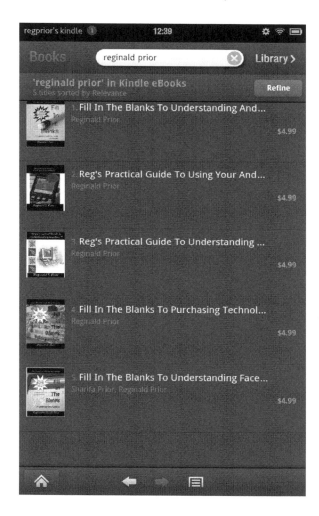

Swipe up or down through the results and single tap the desired book to view a description and to purchase the book. When a book is purchased, it will be downloaded and displayed in the carousel and in the books section with the label "New" on it as shown in the next picture:

You can purchase magazines & newspapers from the "Newsstand" store the same way you would purchase books from the Kindle store.

Reading Books & Other Content On Your Kindle Fire

A lot of additional functionality has been added to the Kindle Fire to make it a great value in the land of tablet computers. But the reason behind having a kindle is to read Electronic Books and magazines. In this section, we will go over how to navigate around E-Books and magazines on the Kindle Fire.

To start reading a E-Book, single tap the "Books" wording on the navigation bar on the home screen. Your bookshelf will come up like the next picture on the left. To start reading a magazine, single tap the "Newsstand" wording. It will come up like the picture on the right:

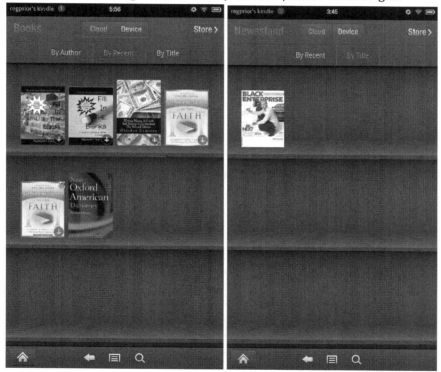

To open a book to read it, single tap a book icon. The book will open and look similar to the next picture on the left. When you single tap a magazine icon, it will look similar to the next picture on the right:

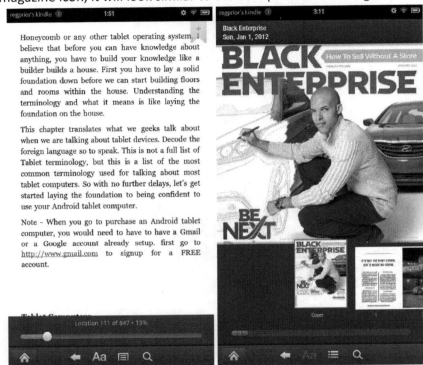

To turn the pages of the book or magazine, swipe left or right across the screen and the pages will turn back or forward. Notice at the bottom of the screen, there are a new set of options for adjusting various settings specifically for reading E-Books and magazines. We will go over those options now in more detail:

- This is the text adjustment menu. Single tap this menu option to see various options for changing the font of your current E-Book among other things as shown in the next picture:

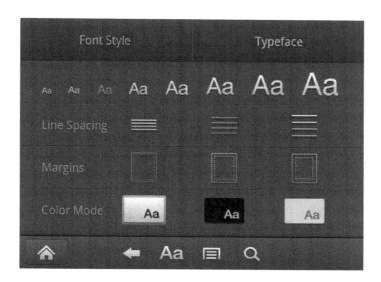

When you are done making changes, single tap the back arrow button to close the menu.

Note – The font adjustment feature is disabled when reading magazines, it is only available in E-Book reading mode.

- The menu key in E-Book mode provides you with E-Book Specific choices such as going to the table of contents. Single tap this button and the menu will come up like the next picture:

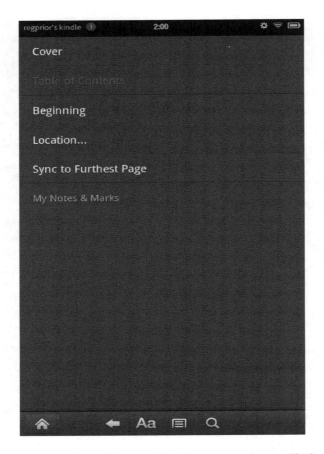

Note – In Magazine reading mode, the menu key will display that specific magazine's table of contents page as shown in the next picture:

Purchasing Items From Amazon With Your Kindle Fire

Amazon is one of the biggest ecommerce and most known global websites ever. Amazon started out life as an online book store. Now Amazon now sells everything from books to shampoo and just about anything else you can think of. You can also use your Kindle fire to purchase non-digital content from Amazon also.

To purchase items from the Amazon Store, on your Favorites bookshelf on the home screen, you will see an icon that looks like the next picture: 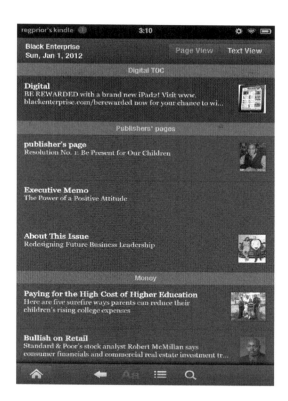This is the Amazon store icon. Single tap this icon to be brought to Amazon's non-digital goods store. It will come up similar to the next picture on the left. You would search through the store to purchase items the same way you would purchase apps & other content by single tapping the "Search For Products" link and typing in what you are searching for. When you wish to see more details on a product, you would single tap that product, and the details screen will come up like the next picture on the right:

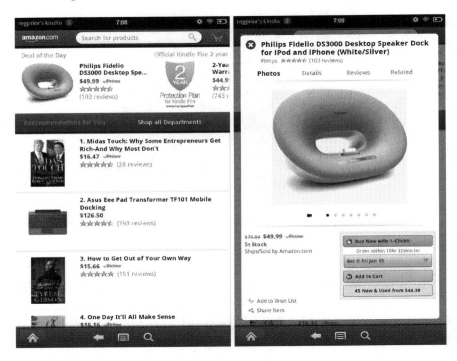

You can purchase this item, add it to your shopping cart, read users reviews on this product or anything else on this screen by single tapping the appropriate buttons. To close this window, single tap the black "X" at the top left part of this screen.

Chapter Four:

Using The Amazon App Market To Add Functionality To Your Kindle Fire

Getting To The Amazon App Market

A lot of buzz words have been circulating about mobile devices for a year or so. But the word "Apps" has been a big one for sure. Apps are short for Application and share the same meaning as with regular computers. Applications are programs designed to perform a function or suite of related functions of benefit to an end user such as email or word processing. On your Kindle Fire, you would get your applications from the Amazon App Market.

To get to the Amazon App Market, on the home screen (You would get to the main screen by pressing the "Home" key from anywhere on your tablet). Single tap the "Apps" menu choice on the navigation bar. The screen will look like the next picture:

You should see on the top right part of this screen a link that says "Store". Single tap the store link, and the Amazon App Store main screen will come up looking like the next picture:

Downloading And Installing Apps

To install an app on your Kindle Fire from the Amazon App Store, there are two ways to do it. The first method is that if you know the name of the app that you want to install, single tap the "Search In Appstore" textbox, and the touch screen keyboard will come up like the next picture.

Type in the name of the app in the search box and single tap the search button on the right side of the keyboard, and the Kindle will search the app store for the app. If the app is available, then it will show up in the results box where you would single tap on it twice to install on your tablet.

In this example, I am going to type in "Piano" to see what piano-related apps are available for the Kindle Fire.

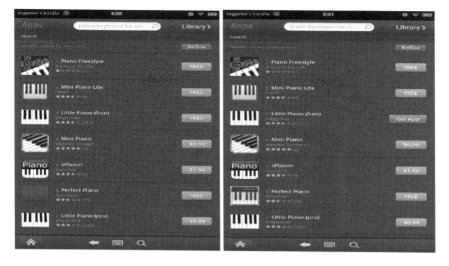

The first screen on the left is the results of the search for piano apps. The screen on the right is where I single tapped one of the piano apps to install it. The button will turn green with the "Get App" wording in the button. Single tap that same button again, then the app will download and install on your Kindle Fire as shown in the next picture:

103

The second way to install apps on your Kindle is to actually look around on the Amazon App Store. Keep in mind that there are thousands of apps on the Amazon App Store and growing every day. The easiest way to do that is when you are at the Amazon App Store main screen, you can single tap a specific category and look through that category for an app that way.

For example, if you were curious about the apps in the entertainment category, single tap the entertainment section and all of the media & video programs that are in the Amazon App Store will show up as shown in the next picture:

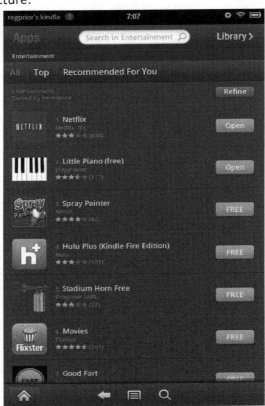

You would swipe up or down to take a look at all of the apps in this category, and when you come across one that interests you, single tap on it twice to install it on your Kindle.

Note – Some apps are free and some are ones that you have to pay for. And the way that you can tell if an app is free or pay is that in on the same line of the app, it would either list "Free" or the cost of the app in US dollars. And if you install the apps that are not free, you would have to purchase them off your credit card through Amazon One-Click.

Another note about apps – Periodically the companies or persons who created the apps you have installed on your tablet releases updates to these apps. To update them, an update icon will appear on your notification menu. Single tap the notification menu, and a menu choice would state that they are updates available for your Kindle. Single tap on that menu choice and all of the updates for the apps will come up.

The apps installed on your tablet that has an update available will be flagged as "Update". To update that app, single tap on the app and a menu will come up for that particular app. Single tap the update button and the app will be updated.

Uninstalling Apps That You Don't Use

From time to time, you may need to clear some space off your Kindle for one reason or another. The best way to clear space on your tablet is to remove apps that you don't use that often.

To remove an app, go to the apps menu on the navigation bar on the home screen (You would get to the home screen by pressing the "Home" key from anywhere on your tablet. It would look like this ) Single tap the "Apps" wording and then all of your installed apps will appear as shown in the next picture:

To uninstall an app, single tap and hold down the icon of the app you wish to uninstall from your Kindle. A pop up menu will come up as shown in the next picture:

On this menu, single tap the "Remove From Device" option, and the uninstall app prompt will come up as shown in the next picture:

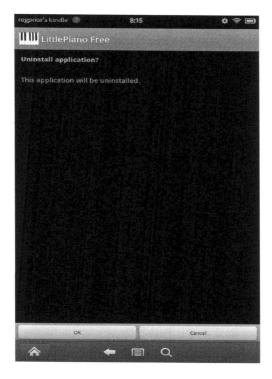

Single tap the "Ok" button, and then the app will be removed from your Kindle.

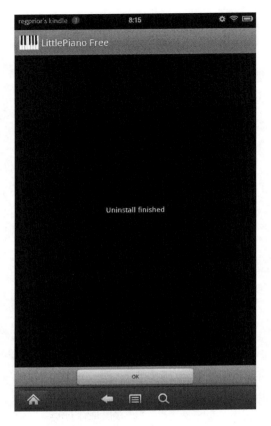

Single tap the "Ok" button to go back to the apps menu.

Chapter Five: Tablet Security

As convenient and easy it is to do many things on your Kindle, the fact remains that your Kindle carries a lot of personal information on it where it could be dangerous if your anyone else who is using your tablet can do something on it where it could adversely affect you in one way or another.

Here are some things you can do to lessen your risk of these things to occur.

1. The first thing you can do to protect your data is to set a screen unlock password. You would do that by going into the quick settings menu by going to the home screen (You would get to the main screen by pressing the "Home" key from anywhere on your tablet. It would look like this ![home])and single tap the battery icon on the top right part of the home screen, then single tap the "more..." option button and the settings menu will come up, looking similar to the next picture:

single tap the "Security" option and the security menu screen will come up like the next picture:

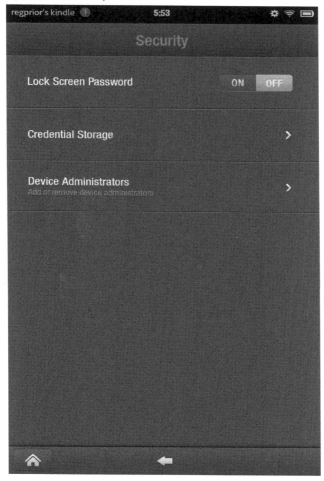

Single tap the "Lock Screen Password" menu option to enable this option, and the screen should look like the next picture:

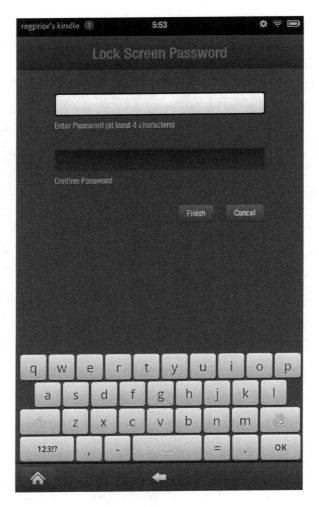

At this screen, enter a password that you can easily remember to unlock your Kindle. After entering your password, single tap the "Finish" button to set the password.

VERY IMPORTANT! – **PLEASE** enter a password that you will not forget because if you enable this option and forget the password, you will not be able to use your Kindle at ALL!

To disable this feature, just go back into the Security menu from the settings menu and single tap the "Lock Screen Password" option again, and the password screen will come up where you would type in your screen unlock password and the feature will be turned off.

2. The second thing you can do is to enable WI-FI restrictions on your Kindle from the settings menu (Especially before giving your Kindle to a child or anyone else!) The reason why I suggest you do this is because anyone can single tap a button to instantly purchase things without your permission (Remember earlier in this book, where we setup the One-Click shopping option for purchasing items?) and charge it to your charge account.

With this option enabled, The Kindle will ask you to enter a password when anything on your Kindle attempts to connect to the Internet to do anything. This in turn lessens the risk of anyone purchasing apps, books or anything else without you knowing about it.

To enable this option, go to the quick settings menu by going to the home screen (You would get to the main screen by pressing the "Home" button from anywhere on your tablet. It would look like this ⌂)and single tap the battery icon on the top right part of the home screen, then single tap the "more..." option button and the settings menu will come up, looking similar to the next picture:

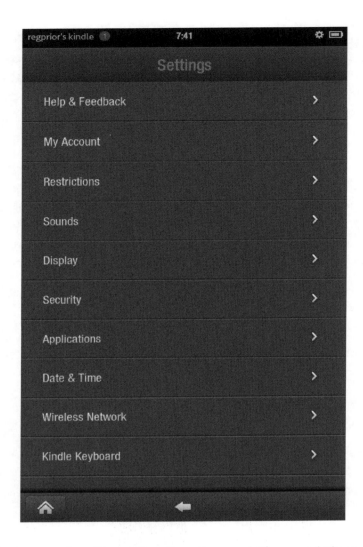

Single tap the "Restrictions" option and the restrictions menu screen will come up like the next picture:

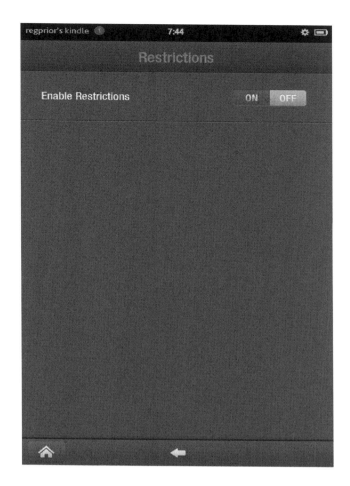

Single tap the "On" link in this menu to turn on the "Enable Restrictions" option and menu will come up asking you to enter a password to enable the feature, looking similar to the next picture:

VERY IMPORTANT! – Please enter a password that you will not forget because if you enable this option and forget the password, you will not be able to use your Internet connection on your Kindle at ALL!

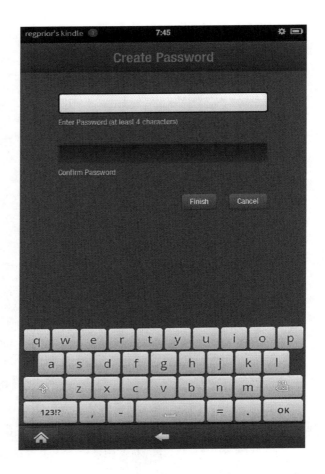

Enter a password in the two textboxes on this screen then single tap the "Finish" button. After you do this, access to your wireless connection will be password protected. Notice on the quick settings section, there is now a key symbol, representing the protected wireless mode as shown in the next picture:

If anyone (including yourself) wishes to access anything on the Internet through your Kindle, your password will need to entered through the quick settings menu to enable the Internet connection as shown in the next picture:

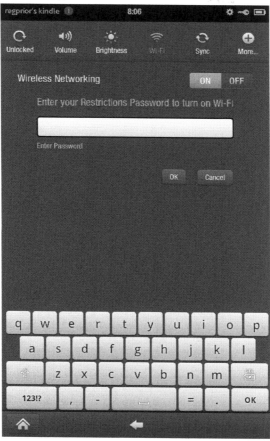

Games, books and other apps already installed on your Kindle's internal memory will work fine, but anything else needing to connect to the Internet (Including Cloud-Based content) will not work until you put in your password to unlock the connection through the quick settings menu.

To disable this option, just go back into the restricted option through the settings menu, and single tap the "Off" option, and the kindle will ask you to enter your password to turn the Wi-Fi restrictions off.

3. The Third thing you can do for Kindle's safety is make sure that you know where you put your Kindle at ALL TIMES!!!

Using a combination or all of these methods listed above will keep your data and your Kindle safe from many threats.

Other Cool Things To Do With Your Kindle Fire

As you can see throughout this entire book, you can do a lot of things with your Kindle Fire. But this chapter is dedicated to showing you the things that you did not know your Kindle Fire can do. So without any more delays, let's get right into it!

The Kindle Fire Can Support Streaming Movies & Television shows from Netflix, Hulu & Pandora!

If you have accounts with any one or all three of these services, then you HAVE to go to the Amazon App Store and download and setup these apps immediately.

You Can Create And Edit Microsoft Office Documents Using A Free App Called Kingsoft Office.

Kingsoft Office is known as the most user-friendly mobile office program. Whether on a small cell phone screen or on a large tablet screen, Kingsoft Office offers the only mobile office app that comes with full-features for FREE!

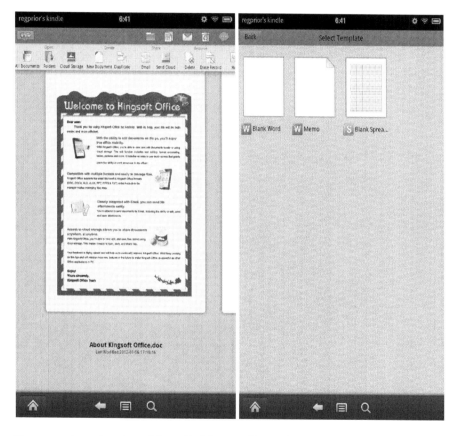

You can download and install this app from the Amazon App Store and start creating and editing Microsoft Office Documents On Your Kindle!

Your Kindle Fire has the ability to print to regular printers using the popular free app EasyPrint and Google's Cloud Print Service.

First, you are going to have Google Chrome Web Browser (located at http://www.google.com/chrome) downloaded and installed on the PC or Mac computer you have printer(s) directly connected to and having the EasyPrint app installed on your Kindle Fire from the Amazon App Store.

Note – Before doing the following steps, you would need to have to have a Gmail or a Google account already setup. First go to http://www.gmail.com to signup for a FREE account.

Open up the Google Chrome web browser on your PC or Mac and the screen should look like the next picture:

Then move your mouse cursor to the settings menu by single left clicking your mouse on the icon which looks like a wrench, and the options menu will come up. Single left click the "Options" link.

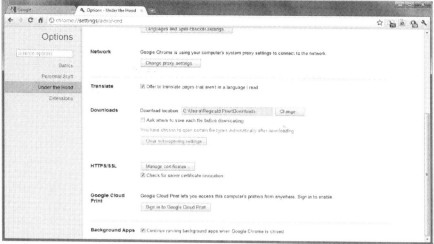

In this menu, single left click the "Under The Hood" wording. After you single clicked the "Under The Hood" option, scroll down to the "Google Cloud Print" option and single left click the "Sign In To Google Cloud Print" button. Next, sign into your Google account and the printer confirmation screen will come up as shown in the next picture:

Single click the Blue "Finish Printer Registration" button and the Thanks page will come up as shown in the next picture:

Now all of your printers that are installed on that computer are now connected to the Google Cloud Print Service and when you single left click the blue "Manage Your Printers" link, you will be taken to the Google Cloud Print main menu as shown in the next picture:

Single left click the "Printers" link on the left side of this screen and a list of all of your printers will show up here. This concludes setting up cloud printing on your computer. The next step is to connect your Kindle to Google's cloud printing service through the EasyPrint App so that you can start printing from your Kindle.

To do this, navigate to the Amazon's App Store and search for "EasyPrint" in the search bar. (If you need detailed instructions on how to download and install apps from the Amazon App Store, refer to page 101) After installing EasyPrint, you will see the EasyPrint Icon in the carousel and the Apps section as shown in the next picture:

Single tap on it and the program will come up as shown in the next picture:

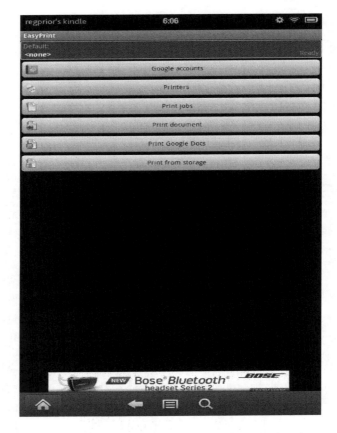

The first thing you have to do upon opening EasyPrint is to add your Google account to the program by single tapping the "Google Accounts" button. The Google Accounts menu will come up similar to the next picture:

Next, single tap the "Add" button at the bottom of this screen and a screen will come up where you would enter your username and password to your Google account as shown in the next picture:

Type in your Google Account username and password, then single tap the "Login" button to connect to Google's Cloud Print service. Single tap the back arrow key to go back to the main menu.

Next, we have to select a default printer for EasyPrint to use when printing documents or anything else from our Kindle Fire. Single tap the "Printers" button, and all of your printers that was loaded to Google's Cloud print will be listed here as shown in the next picture:

To select one of these printers as the default printer, single tap on one of them. In this example, I am going to select my Canon D400 printer. When you do that, the Default setting at the top of this menu will change from <none> to the Canon Printer. After selecting a printer from this menu, single tap the back arrow button to go back to the main menu. At this point, we are ready to select a document to print to our printer from our Kindle Fire!

To actually print a saved document on the Kindle, single tap the "Print Document" button, and then you will be taken to the main directory on the Kindle's internal memory as shown in the next picture:

Earlier I had created a document in Kingsoft Office that I wish to print. This program saves all documents in the "Documents" folder. So I single tap on that folder to open it and view the document as shown in the next picture:

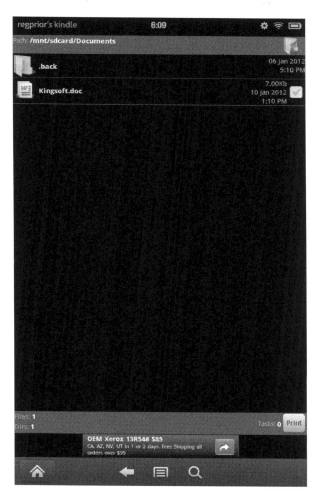

To print the document, single tap the checkbox on the right side of the document to choose it, then single tap the "Print" button. The document will be sent to your printer. To go back to the previous folder, single tap the Folder icon where it states ".back" and you will go back to the previous folder.

Note – It will take anywhere from 30 seconds to 1 minute for the document to start actually printing. That is because the document has to be transferred from your Kindle to the Google Cloud Print Service and then to your printer.

I hope that you have gained a lot of knowledge in learning more about your Kindle Fire by reading this book. Just like in the preface, you are the most important critic and value all of your feedback about this book so that I can improve future texts. Thank you for reading and look forward to hearing from you!!

Made in the USA
San Bernardino, CA
26 April 2016